Original title:
Scarves of Serendipity

Copyright © 2025 Creative Arts Management OÜ
All rights reserved.

Author: Liam Sterling
ISBN HARDBACK: 978-1-80586-015-0
ISBN PAPERBACK: 978-1-80586-487-5

Unexpected Wraps

In a world of threads so wild,
Lost my way like a wandering child.
A twist here, a tangle there,
Now I'm wearing my dog's hair!

Fluffy fabric, bright and bold,
He thought it was a treasure to hold.
Now I trip over styles I own,
Fashion advice? I just groan.

The Loom of Destiny

At the loom fate took a turn,
What was gold? Now I discern.
A snazzy wrap for a night out,
Turned into a napper's clout!

Thread by thread, I weave my fate,
One moment stylish, next I wait.
Bumping into folks with flair,
While they stare at my mismatched wear.

Patterns in the Wind

Caught a breeze, oh what a thrill,
Flaps like a flag, against my will.
My wrap takes flight, a bird so free,
Land on a friend who laughs at me!

Colors clash, and spots don't match,
A rainbow mess, what a fine patch!
Dancing fabric, swirling spins,
With every gust, it once again wins.

Knots of Providence

Tied up tight in life's big plan,
Grabbed a knot and ran like a fan.
On my way to a fashion show,
Tripped, fell, and stole the show though!

Tangled threads, a comical sight,
People giggle, but it feels right.
Laughter echoes, fun on display,
Who needs style anyway?

Winding Trails of Wonder

On paths where laughter weaves and spins,
I tripped on a rogue knot of whims.
The world twirled with a silly flair,
As squirrels donned hats made of air.

A tumble here, a giggle there,
My feet danced lightly, without a care.
Each step was an accidental jest,
In a wacky world where fun is best.

The Gift of Twisted Threads

A ball of yarn rolled on the floor,
It tangled toes that asked for more.
A puppy joined the playful spree,
Creating chaos, oh what glee!

With every loop and every twist,
The laughter grew, it couldn't be missed.
A knitted sock, a quirky hat,
Unexpected joy, imagine that!

Threads of Chance

In the cupboard where dust bunnies cheer,
I found a thread that pulled me near.
A string of fate, a twist of chance,
It led me straight to a sock puppet dance.

With every tug, new faces appeared,
In a revelry that was utterly weird.
Each puppet spoke in rhymes so bold,
Sharing tales of adventures untold.

Woven Whispers

In the corner, a tapestry glows,
With whispered secrets that everyone knows.
Threads from a clown, a cat, and a bee,
All come together in a raucous spree.

The stitches giggle, the colors collide,
As they plot a mischief-filled ride.
A fabric of fun, with frays and loops,
Where hilarity grows in whimsical troops.

The Unexpected Wrap

A twist of fabric, oh so bold,
It wraps me tightly, truth be told.
I thought it was a fancy cape,
But now I look like a potato shape.

I strut around, I trip and slide,
While giggles echo far and wide.
My outfit's wild, a comical sight,
But hey, I'm cozy and feeling quite bright.

Threads of Delight

A flick of thread, a splash of hue,
I thought I'd charm with something new.
Instead, I look like a walking mess,
Clashing patterns—oh, what a guess!

Yet laughter spills from every glance,
As friends all gather, eager to dance.
In this riot of colors, I shine so bold,
Embracing the joy, letting go of cold.

Cozy Knots of Joy

A knot here, a knot there with crafty flair,
I planned a chic look, a stylish affair.
But oh dear me, what have I done?
I'm tangled and jumbled, not having fun!

Yet laughter erupts like a joyous song,
As I spin around, I can't be wrong.
In this fabric fiesta, who needs a clue?
For joy's in the dancing—come join the zoo!

Embracing the Unforeseen

A lopsided wrap, a snazzy flair,
I thought I'd impress, but who really cares?
My scarf's a creature of whims and dreams,
Taking on forms that burst at the seams.

In every twist, a giggle erupts,
As friends all cheer, 'Oh look, she's stumped!'
I may not win fashion's high regard,
But wrap me in laughter, I'll play the bard.

Entwined Fates

In a twist, I stole your wrap,
You chased me through the night gap.
Laughter echoed in the breeze,
A dance of threads, if you please.

You tripped, I fell, a clumsy twirl,
We tangled in fabric, oh what a whirl!
A scarf in hand, or was it two?
Who knew fate came with a fashion clue?

Giggling, we forgot the strife,
Two tangled souls in a jumbled life.
Fashion faux pas or fate's intention,
Creating joy in this odd invention.

The Blessing of Fabric

A pashmina blessed by the wise,
Wrapped it around my friend with sighs.
It fluttered off like a bird,
Chasing laughter, oh how absurd!

Fabric flew, and so did glee,
As it caught on the neighbor's tea.
A grand display of colors bright,
Knitted chaos in the soft moonlight.

We giggled as we tugged and pulled,
While the neighbor looked thoroughly fooled.
"Is it a curtain or a flag?" we cried,
In the tapestry of joy, we gladly abide.

Unexpected Echoes

A scarf slipped off in the café line,
Danced with grace, it felt divine.
Slipped on a muffin, rolled in jam,
Our laughter echoed—what a sham!

Who knew dessert could behave so sly?
Wearing crumbs, we couldn't lie.
Our heads threw back, a joyful spree,
A bakery brawl, oh the irony!

Each fabric twirl became a tale,
As we paraded, hearts set sail.
Life wrapped in layers, silly and grand,
In this chaos, forever we'll stand.

Under the Fabric of Chance

Beneath a layer of colorful cloth,
Chance chuckled while we took an oath.
To wear our quirks like a crown,
In this wild world, we won't back down.

Each tangled thread, a story spun,
We danced like fools, oh what fun!
A pop of colors, and we collide,
In this playground, we take each stride.

Life's draped in humor, stitched with flair,
Unexpected moments float in the air.
With every twist, our hearts might leap,
Under chance's quilt, our joy runs deep.

Unraveled Mysteries

In a drawer, tangled threads play,
A knit so wild, it leads astray.
Colors clash in a vibrant dance,
Who knew yarn could take a chance?

One sock leans left, the other right,
A pair? Not quite, what a sight!
The cat gets caught in the loop,
Now it thinks it's part of the troupe.

Textures of Bliss

Silken strands in a happy twist,
Each weave tells tales that can't be missed.
A tangle here, a knot so true,
A fabric of fun in every hue.

I drape it on, feel the cheer,
Turns my frowns to laughter near.
A wrap that hugs my silly smirk,
Laughing at life's little quirk.

Embracing the Unforeseen

Who knew a scarf could bring such glee?
It's caught in the door, oh woe is me!
It swirls and twirls like a wily breeze,
Yet it giggles softly as it frees.

A fashion faux pas, but darling too,
In every mishap, there's joy for you.
A floppy end waves like a greeting,
In the world of blunders, it's still competing.

The Silk of Serendipity

A fabric of fate hangs on a hook,
One tug leads to laughter, come take a look!
It drapes in styles not meant to be,
Fashion advice? Just let it be free.

Patterns that clash, oh what a sight,
My friends all chuckle, oh what a fright!
Yet in the chaos, joy I find,
In every twist, I'm truly aligned.

Elysian Wraps

In winter's chill, a twist of fate,
A tangled thread, we celebrate.
With patterns bright, and colors bold,
We wrap ourselves in stories told.

A mishap here, a knot made tight,
Yet laughter comes, it's pure delight.
We dance around, a merry band,
In breezy parks, we take a stand.

When friends collide, oh what a sight,
Our antics shared, through day and night.
We drape our dreams on sunny days,
In whimsical, adventurous ways.

The Echo of Fortune

A playful breeze, a twisty kite,
As life unfolds, we find the light.
With each wild toss, a chance we find,
In laughter's echo, we unwind.

A chance encounter, a hat askew,
Fortune chuckles, and so do you.
With every flap, in bright array,
Our fate entwined, come what may.

Like laundry hung on sunny lines,
Our fortunes dance, as laughter shines.
A funny hat and frumpy shoes,
In life's grand play, it's how we choose.

Woven Journeys

In markets vibrant, the colors fly,
We trade our tales as time goes by.
With twinkling eyes and playful jest,
We weave the threads, a fancy fest.

Each knot a giggle, each loop a cheer,
Adventures shared, we hold them dear.
With friends beside, our spirits soar,
In every twist, we crave for more.

Through winding paths and endless trails,
Our laughter echoes and never fails.
We wrap our hearts in bright designs,
In silly moments, that fate aligns.

Tidal Threads

The ocean calls with rippling sound,
As we chase waves on sandy ground.
A flip-flop gone, a tumble too,
In salty air, our joy shines through.

With every purl, a splash and cheer,
We spin around, without a fear.
The sunlit sea, a playful tease,
We dance with glee, as we please.

A seagull swoops, with antics grand,
In clumsy joy, we make our stand.
Our swirling tales with every tide,
In laughter's wave, we take a ride.

Threads That Bind

In a tangled mess of yarn,
Knots meet laughter, who'd have thought?
Jumbled fibers dance around,
Crafting tales of what we caught.

A stitch here, a snip up there,
Nothing is quite as it seems.
We weave our stories unaware,
Life's fabric's stronger than dreams.

With every twist, a chuckle grows,
Each loop, a tale of fate's delight.
Colors clash, but friendship glows,
Knitting joy through day and night.

So come unwind and share a thread,
Laugh at mishaps, stitch by stitch.
In our creation, there's no dread,
Just the joy of our little glitch.

Colors of Coincidence

A burst of hues in a funky hat,
Orange and purple, what's the plan?
Worn proudly, hey, imagine that!
A rainbow giggles at our tan.

Spilled coffee on a bright pink scarf,
A patch of laughter stains the day.
Each drop a pattern, pure and soft,
Creating joy in quirky ways.

Fate's palette spills across the street,
Bumping into socks worn mismatched.
With each collision, life's a treat,
Our quirky colors safely hatched.

So let's embrace this artful jest,
With stripes of love that never fade.
In each weird twist, we are blessed,
In serendipity, we've played.

Frayed Edges of Life

Life's seams are frayed, a little worn,
Like my old coat, still on my back.
Laughing at the days forlorn,
Threadbare patches mark our track.

Stitches pop, a whimsical show,
Who knew fray could bring a grin?
Loosely knitted joy does flow,
Every snag, a tale within.

Wander 'round in shabby threads,
Each snag a laugh, each rip a cheer.
Weaving joy in loose instead,
Finding treasure far and near.

So let's parade our frayed attire,
With patchwork hearts and funny style.
In the quirks of life, we conspire—
To keep on laughing all the while.

The Cloak of Clarity

Wrapped in fabric, thoughts unwind,
Mysteries fade in cozy folds.
Underneath this cloak, we find,
Life's odd moments brightly tolds.

Mismatched patterns, a fashion spree,
Questions answered 'neath the seams.
In silly threads, we find the key,
Laughter's warmth turns doubts to dreams.

When life feels heavy, just cocoon,
In fabric woven with our quirks.
With every giggle, night or noon,
We let go of the silly jerks.

So let us twirl in this grand wrap,
Casting shadows on all our fears.
In the cloak's laughter, take a nap,
With threads of joy throughout the years.

Tapestry of Connections

In a room full of hats, a sock found a shoe,
Dancing together, they spun a bright hue.
Laughter erupted, as tops tumbled down,
A bow tie declared, "Look at us now!"

A coat made of laughter and pockets of cheer,
Joined the parade with a wig and a sneer.
Buttons were bouncing, they filled up the air,
Unlikely friendships, a spontaneous pair.

Under the table with crumbs on the floor,
A mitten and glove found an open door.
With giggles contagious, they rolled through the hall,
Together they shouted, "We're having a ball!"

Every stitch woven a tale of delight,
Embroidered with joy, glowing ever so bright.
In a world made of fabric, connections unfold,
Through threads of pure humor, we're rich as gold.

Unexpected Tints

A yellow polka dot met a plaid just in time,
Hatching a plan that was utterly prime.
With spots and with stripes, they painted the town,
Creating a canvas where wiggles astound.

Persuading a camper, a bright hiking vest,
To join in their shenanigans, simply the best.
Together they floundered through colors so stark,
They turned quite a few heads at the local park.

A rainbow of socks spilled out from a drawer,
Each one a character wanting to explore.
With giggles and mischief, they danced on the floors,
Creating a whirlpool of soft fabric roars.

As they rattled and rolled, the colors turned bold,
Each hue a confetti of treasure to hold.
In this fabric carnival, laughter ensues,
Unexpectedly vivid in all the right hues.

Fabrics of Discovery

An apron from Grandma, a story to tell,
Rescued from dust in a delightful spell.
With flour on the counter, it twirled with a grin,
Whisking up tales, oh, let the fun begin!

A patchwork of moments, each square a delight,
Stitched together with giggles that light up the night.
With scissors in hand, they dared to create,
An ensemble of mischief, oh, it had to wait!

One thread had a vision, a quirky design,
While another was stuck in a loop quite divine.
Through yarns of confusion, they knitted a play,
Unraveled their worries, tossed gloom far away.

With each little patch, they discovered anew,
Friendships were woven like fabric they drew.
In laughter and colors, they found a way in,
A tapestry vibrant with joy and with sin.

A Stitch in Time

A needle in hand and a button to flaunt,
Set forth on adventures, a whimsical jaunt.
With threads of mischief, they crafted a scene,
Where socks held debates on where they had been.

A tape measure chimed in with tales of its claim,
It stretched and it wriggled, it never felt fame.
The fabric of friendship wrapped tight with a cheer,
Sewing up moments that bring warmth and clear.

A patch on the knee, a hole in the seam,
Turned into a saga, a stitch in a dream.
With laughter infectious, they sewed through the night,
Creating a quilt of affection and light.

So next time you're mending, or perhaps just to chill,
Remember the threads that weave laughter and thrill.
In stitches and smiles, we'll find the old rhyme,
Sewing our stories, a stitch in good time.

The Weave of Discovery

In a corner store, a plaid surprise,
Found a tangled mess before my eyes.
Tried to wear it, looked quite absurd,
The clerk just laughed and said a word.

I wrapped it once, around my head,
Like a pirate, mischief widespread.
Each twist and turn, a tale to find,
Every look was fun, never maligned.

A neighbor thought I joined a cult,
With every knot, my style would jolt.
Imagine the giggles, what a delight,
Creating joy from a fabric fight.

Now every color brings a cheer,
Every pattern giggles, nothing to fear.
In the fabric's dance, we spin and prance,
Life's crazy weave, our chance to enhance.

The Rainbow of Serendipity

Found a garish piece in the thrift store aisle,
Funky colors to make anyone smile.
Tried it on, looked like a clown,
But hey, who wouldn't want to wear a frown?

A swirl of hues that laugh and sing,
Wearing it brings the spring-like zing.
Socks, a hat, and now a wrap,
All mismatched, but I'm in the lap.

Someone shouted, 'What a sight!'
I twirled around, feeling so bright.
Jeans and sneakers, what a pair,
Prancing like I just don't care.

The world became my catwalk stage,
Every step, a new fun page.
In rainbow colors, I'm bold, I'm brave,
In funny threads, my laughter waves.

Emblems of Unforeseen

A forgotten shawl that held some dust,
Longing for wear, it's a fabric must.
Draped it on, felt like a queen,
Turns out I'm a stylish machine!

A friend popped in, laughed at first glance,
"Chic or shabby?" we took a chance.
With every twist, a giggle swirled,
Unexpected fun, in my fabric world.

Worn inside out, it spiced the scene,
Looked like a superhero, fresh and keen.
What once was lost now steals the gaze,
In those threads, I'm lost in a daze.

Each flap and fold has tales to tell,
Even the llamas would giggle and yell.
In patterns wild, life's odd little games,
With laughs and joy, it makes us feel famous.

Unsought Elegance

A crumpled piece from the kitchen drawer,
Looks like it's traveled the world and more.
Tossed it on, and oh what fun,
I'm the life of the party, everyone!

What a sight, peeked in the mirror,
Fashionable bloopers never clearer.
Each wear a story, goofy, unique,
Strutting around, I'm a high-fashion freak!

"Is that a haute couture trend?"
Friends giggle wide and then they bend.
Twirling, dancing, all carefree,
In my frumpy glory, I'm truly free.

From kitchen cloth to runways above,
In these antics, I find the love.
Life's a canvas, paint it bright,
With wit and charm, I shine the light.

Unraveled Journeys

In the closet a dance, they twist and twirl,
Lurking in layers, a colorful swirl.
A journey of threads, they weave and spin,
Where did that one go? Oh, let the fun begin!

On a chilly day, one slipped from my grasp,
It took off in style, oh what a gasp!
A rogue fashion statement, it waved from afar,
Chasing it down like a lost shooting star.

Over cups of cocoa, they gossip and scheme,
Trading old stories, like a wild dream.
But knots get quite tangled, oh what a mess,
An untimely slapstick, I must confess!

So here's to the twists that life will impart,
To colors and patterns that warm the heart.
In laughter and joy, each thread brings delight,
Unraveled journeys that spark pure twilight.

Interlaced Echoes

Quietly lounging, a dandy parade,
A mish-mash of colors from cool to charade.
They chatter and giggle, oh what a crowd,
All the mismatched parts, they dance fierce and proud.

When one trips over, chaos ensues,
An intricate weaving of shock and amuse.
Not a fashion faux pas, just a joyful slip,
They tumble and roll like a group on a trip.

Nestled in pockets, a stray thread was found,
Paired with a pattern, they twirled all around.
An echo of laughter, a fabric affair,
Their interlaced dreams float lightly in the air.

A honeycomb twist, life's puns have their place,
With warmth all around, they're wrapped in embrace.
A riot of color, they frolic and thrive,
In funny connections, they keep dreams alive.

The Cozy Convergence

On a bustling street, a tumble begins,
Like a dog and a cat, or a pair of lost twins.
One socks it to me, a hat joins the fray,
A cozy convergence, brightening the day.

A whirl of textures and playful delight,
Each piece finding home in the colorful light.
"Who wore it best?" a question so dire,
As they trickle like rivers, or dance on a wire.

When the drizzle hits, they cluster for warmth,
Huddled like penguins, they smile and they charm.
Though mismatched and wobbly, their spirits are high,
In this wacky parade, who needs to comply?

Together they laugh at the odd way they blend,
With a wink and a nod, they don't need to pretend.
A cozy convergence, where magic is spun,
In funny companionship, together we run.

Soft Embraces of Coincidence

A flurry of moments, like whispers in time,
Soft embraces that tickle, like a silly rhyme.
With colors confetti, they float through the air,
Unexpected encounters, without a single care.

In the warmth of a café, they greet with a cheer,
Sipping on stories, laughter's near.
Questionable choices, but oh-so appealing,
An ironic embrace, a joy that's revealing.

At the bus stop one morning, a scarf took a leap,
Chasing a pigeon, oh what a heap!
With a chuckle and grin, a heart full of glee,
Soft coincidences, wild as can be.

So let's twirl in this dance, in circles we tread,
Finding fun in the places that life's laughter led.
With every mishap and twist, we enter the dream,
In soft embraces, we're all part of the scheme.

Driftwood and Dreams

On the beach, a guy found a shoe,
He slipped it on, What else could he do?
A frisbee flew high, lost in the tides,
He chased it with laughter, his pride he bides.

A driftwood wand, oh what a sight,
He waved it around, igniting delight.
Seagulls squawked tunes, from up in the sky,
As he twirled and danced, oh my, oh my!

Caught in a moment, sand in his toes,
A crab claimed his foot, a surprise no one knows.
With giggles and sand, fortunes collude,
A silly escapade, like a kid's interlude.

As sunset crept in, casting red light,
He waved to the sky, what a funny sight!
With driftwood and dreams, absurdity reigns,
In every lost shoe, laughter remains.

Twists of Fortune

A lady lost her hat, a gust did betray,
It flew past a dog, who thought it was play.
Chasing it round, with all of his might,
They danced through the park, a comical sight.

Old men by the bench, shared a gleeful look,
As hats led a chase, like a plot from a book.
The pup claimed his prize, with a playful bow,
But the lady just laughed, calling, "Hey, that's my cow!"

Round and around, the antics unwind,
Twists of misfortune, yet joy intertwined.
A hat and a dog, a friendship ignites,
In the chaos of life, what a marvelous flight!

So here's to the trips, where laughter ascends,
In twisted adventures, we find furry friends.
With hats gone astray, mischief decorates,
Life's funny surprises, our hearts celebrate.

Veils of Joy

A clown in a park, bright colors galore,
Balanced on stilts, he teeters and soars.
Children erupt with contagious delight,
As he juggles with pies, an outrageous sight.

A lady in pink, with balloons on her dress,
Tripped on a vine, oh what a mess!
She laughed as she tumbled, her joy uncontained,
In veils of sheer giggles, the laughter remained.

An ice cream cart rolled, what a splashed scene,
With flavors like pickle, and broccoli green.
Yet everyone cheered, what a curious treat,
In the merry mayhem, life tasted sweet!

So here's to the jesters, the whimsy they bring,
In laughter's bright web, oh how we shall sing.
Veils of joy floating, in sunshine and cheer,
In this silly world, we find love without fear.

Cascading Connections

A man dropped his phone in a puddle so wide,
Out leaped a frog, with a leap and a glide.
It plopped on his lap, with a croak and a glee,
"Oh what a moment! This isn't just me!"

A dog chased the frog, what chaos ensued,
Through gardens and flowerbeds, all were imbued.
With giggles from passersby, full of delight,
Cascading connections, oh what a sight!

A woman with cookies joined in the fray,
She tossed treats about, what a lovely display.
The frog hopped for biscuits, the dog for some fun,
In this wild scene of joy, no need to outrun!

So here's to the mishaps, the joy that they bring,
In puddles and laughter, life's a peculiar fling.
With connections all around, an echoing cheer,
In chaos and frolic, the heart draws near.

Stitches of Fortune

In a bustling cafe, a knot appears,
A twist of yarn, shared laughs and cheers.
A poodle in stripes, tries to blend in,
But trips on the thread, oh where to begin!

A squirrel with style, a hat on his head,
Picks up the yarn, and scurries ahead.
He crafts a bouquet, from a sock on the floor,
A fashionista now, oh what a lore!

Grandma's old scarf flutters in glee,
A tangled mess becomes pure art, you see.
Scissors, and threads, a magical spree,
Who knew fortune's stitched quite so carefree?

Stitches and giggles, a rainbow so bright,
Every misstep leads to sheer delight.
In this patchwork world, where quirks intertwine,
Laughing at fate, our fortunes align!

Twists of Fate

In a shop of whimsy, the oddest of things,
A slip of a ribbon, a tie that just sings.
The cat in a bow tie, purring with cheer,
Detangles the mess, as if it were clear.

Two mismatched mittens, a scandalous sight,
One for the left, the other, the right.
They dance on the table, chaotically free,
Who knew that lost socks could lead to such glee?

The mustached penguin wobbles with flair,
With a pie on his head, he's quite unaware.
He slips on a patch of misplaced yarn,
With a twirl and a giggle, he manages charm.

Twists and turns in this maze of fun,
Where every faux pas shines brighter than sun.
In the fabric of fate, where stories elope,
We find our own paths, while crafting our hope!

Woven Dreams

Once a tangle of colors, a dream gone awry,
Weaves tales of wonder, as laughter draws nigh.
A llama in plaid, prances through town,
Knitting a scarf that's the talk of the gown.

A goat in a beanie, pulls at some thread,
Surprises all onlookers as it hops ahead.
With a wink and a nod, he gathers a crowd,
Creating connections, both silly and loud.

Underneath the moon, a mishmash of sights,
With twinkling mishaps, and laughter-filled nights.
Giggling at knots that refuse to let go,
In the woven fabric, new adventures still flow.

Woven together, laughter so sweet,
With dreams in our hands, we dance to the beat.
The tapestry grows, rich with delight,
In this fanciful world, everything feels right!

The Dance of Destiny

In a party of socks, a balletic affair,
Each one takes a chance, twirling in the air.
A fabulous mismatch, the crowd gasps in awe,
As a polka-dot sock breaks out in a flaw!

The tango of turtlenecks spins round and round,
With every step forward, bizarre turns abound.
A squirrel in a tutu leads with great style,
As all the lost gloves join in with a smile.

Jigs of the jaunty, and pirouettes too,
All stitching together in a kooky debut.
The stage is set, with an unexpected cast,
In this playful gala, memories are vast.

Laughter erupts with each dance elite,
Where every odd pairing makes life bittersweet.
In this symphony bright with jumps and with spins,
We discover with joy, where the heart truly wins!

Threads of Chance

In the closet, colors clash,
Where mismatched socks all dash.
Tiny threads weave fate's delight,
Laughing softly, oh what a sight!

The cat's found a yarn to chase,
Twirling 'round in a wild race.
Every loop, a twist of jest,
Is this the thread that fits us best?

Fumbling fingers, tangled fun,
Knots and giggles, we've just begun!
Life's a fabric, stitched with care,
We wear our awkwardness to share.

In tangled threads, we find our way,
Through curly paths, we laugh and play.
Each silly knot a tale well-spun,
An adventure shared, two hearts as one.

Whispers in the Fabric

A patchwork quilt of goofy dreams,
Threads whisper softly, or so it seems.
In every stitch, a secret lives,
From tangled tales, the laughter gives.

Laughter echoes through the seams,
As I sew my patchy schemes.
Each fabric piece, a story told,
In colorful tones, both bright and bold.

Fingers busy, hearts in sync,
Stitching laughter as we think.
Woven tales of silly chance,
In twirly patterns, we laugh and dance.

From cotton to some shiny silk,
Our antics flow like creamy milk.
Soft threads join us hand in hand,
In this fabric land, we make our stand.

Tangles of the Heart

Two hearts wrapped in a big old hug,
Twisting threads like a cozy rug.
With every knot, we share a grin,
In love's tapestry, let fun begin!

Our yarn gets tangled, oh what a mess,
But we just laugh, it's all for the best.
In every loop, a giggle grows,
With each little twist, our mischief shows.

We're knitting dreams with silly flair,
As patchy moments fill the air.
Each tangled stitch a story we weave,
In this fabric life, we both believe.

Though yarn may fray, our hearts stay tight,
In every twist, we find the light.
Through ups and downs, we'll always lark,
In this playful dance, we leave our mark.

The Knitted Pathways

In the park, a yarn ball rolls,
As laughter bubbles, filling our souls.
Around the bench, the kids all play,
Dropping stitches in such a funny way!

Threads of fate can tangle and weave,
Sometimes they bind us, yet we believe.
With each little knot, we twist and shout,
In this colorful maze, we leap about.

Patterns form like silly jokes,
In every stitch, our joy evokes.
With laughter's thread, we're never lost,
In this knitted world, we bear the cost.

So let us weave, in cheeky threads,
With every loop where laughter spreads.
The pathways knit both near and far,
Bring us together, a shining star.

Hold Onto Happiness

In the closet, a mess awaits,
Colors tangled in playful fates,
A scarf of plaid, with polka dots,
Wrap it right, forget the knots.

Twist it here, and tie it there,
A fashion statement, who would dare?
With every loop, a giggle grows,
Catching smiles wherever it goes.

Fringe and laughter dance in the breeze,
Chasing fun like children with ease,
Oh, what a sight in a silly hue,
A joyful knot to start anew!

So hold on tight, don't let it slip,
Let whimsy be your friendship sip,
Beneath the layers of every fold,
Happiness found, like stories told.

Threads of Delight

Woven whims with a twisty flair,
Silly colors, beyond compare,
A pink and green, a shocking sight,
Don't judge me now, it feels just right!

A cotton square for my head I place,
Look at me now, a fashion grace!
With every glance, a burst of cheer,
More laughter brewed with every sneer.

Knots and bows are my favorite game,
Confetti vibes with a dance of fame,
Each thread a tale, a giggling prance,
Dancing in circles, a joyous chance!

So let's spin round, and let's unwind,
In colors wild, we leave woes behind,
Laughter grows like a sprawling vine,
With threads of joy, we brightly shine.

Chance's Embrace in the Wind

A wild gust steals my bright attire,
Chasing dreams like an endless fire,
This bright shawl, it flutters and flies,
My own little kite reaching for the skies!

A knot here and there, who needs a plan?
Swirling colors make me feel grand,
The universe giggles, oh what a thrill,
As chance winks, I do a cartwheel!

Funny how fate can tickle one's heart,
With every twist, a jaunt, a start,
Serendipity laughs with every bound,
In the chaotic dance where joy is found!

Twist and twirl, we weave through the haze,
With a cheeky grin, let's embrace the craze,
For in every flurry, there's magic to find,
In the breeze of chance and a state of mind.

Mystical Textures

In a drawer of wonders, I pulled it out,
A fabric so fine, I couldn't live without.
It danced on my neck like it had a dream,
But tied itself up—oh, what a scheme!

A twist and a turn, it tangled my hair,
My cat gave a grin—was it love or a dare?
It flutters and flaps in the breeze of delight,
Ready for laughter, it takes to the night.

Colors that tangle, they tease and they laugh,
Turning the mundane into a quick photograph.
Every fold tells a tale that tickles the soul,
It's a whimsical journey, let's roll on a scroll!

So wrap it around, let's make it a game,
Who dressed like a clown? Oh, it's you! What a name!
In the realm of the quirky, it reigns as a star,
With a wink and a giggle, we'll travel afar.

Unseen Embraces

Once hid in the closet, a phantom so bright,
It whispered of journeys beneath the moonlight.
With a flick and a twirl, it caught me unaware,
An embrace from the shadows—a soft, funny affair!

When I stepped out in public, the giggles were loud,
I looked like a butterfly lost in a crowd.
"Oh dear, what a sight!" as I walked through the park,
A creature of laughter, I lit up the dark.

A hug from the past wrapped tight around me,
With every twist, a new laugh set free.
The friends all around me, they chuckled with glee,
In this cloak of giggles, everyone agrees!

So here's to the charm of the hidden and shy,
That brings out the joy as it flutters by.
Life's a parade of the unforeseen fun,
Let's twirl with the quirks until day is done.

Harmonious Bindings

With notes in the fabric, a melody spun,
Tangled in laughter, my day's just begun.
Dancing through alleys where giggles take flight,
This binding of joy wraps me up tight.

A knot here, a loop there, a symphony plays,
I'm serenaded by whimsy in so many ways.
It flutters and spins, an eccentric ballet,
In the opera of clumsiness, I take center stage.

Strangers stop to snicker, they join in the dance,
A jester's parade, will you take a chance?
So we waddle and wiggle, creating a scene,
In the fabric of fate, we're all part of the dream!

Let's gather our laughter, our quirks, and our ties,
In the tapestry woven, each silly surprise.
With harmonious laughter, we'll carry the cheer,
Together we sparkle—joy's always near!

The Workshop of Wishes

In a cozy old workshop, the dreams start to hum,
With materials swirling, like sugar and gum.
Crafting creations with laughter and flair,
Each twist holds a secret, each stitch, a dare!

Buttons and fabric, they chatter and sway,
"Make me a tickler!" they giggle and play.
I knotted up mischief, oh what a delight,
Even the tools seem to smile in the light.

One moment, a cap; the next, a bright scarf,
A comical token to fill hearts with mirth.
As I snip and I sew, the wishes take flight,
In this vibrant collage, we ignite the night.

So let's gather our dreams, in this magical room,
Where giggles are whispers that brightly consume.
With each twinkle of laughter, a wish in the air,
In the workshop of whimsy—let's happily share!

Embraces Beyond Desire

In a shop of mismatched cloth,
Where colors dance and giggles froth,
Two fellows chose a shade of green,
To match a hat that he had seen.

They twirled and twisted, bright in glee,
A fabric fight for all to see,
With every fold, a chuckle loud,
As they became a vibrant crowd.

A twist, a turn, a snip of thread,
With laughter spilling—lightly spread,
The look on Grandma's face was grand,
A masterpiece from mishaps planned.

But who knew that a simple whim,
Would lead to such a fashion hymn?
Their hearts entwined beyond the thread,
In a tapestry of joy, they wed.

Unexpected Stitches

A tailor's cat, in youthful play,
Pounced on fabric every day,
Knocking buttons left and right,
Creating chaos—what a sight!

The seams began to live and breathe,
Each patch a story to bequeath,
Two pockets mismatched on a vest,
Each holding secrets—quite a jest!

A rip, a tear, and then a flare,
Those fashion faux pas hung in air,
With friends around, they all would sing,
How odd is charm in everything!

They strutted through the town with pride,
And chuckled at their joyful side,
For every flaw was just the prime,
To turn mistakes into pure rhyme.

The Quilt of Discovery

A blanket made of every care,
With patches bold, they dared to share,
Each snippet told of how they fell,
In love with laughter, oh so well!

From dances by the kitchen sink,
To spilled tea that made them think,
The quilt was stitched with every cheer,
A symbol of their bonds held dear.

With buttons from a first date night,
And stitches done in sheer delight,
They found that memories can bind,
A funny quilt with love aligned.

In every corner, stories bloom,
Of mishaps spun in cozy room,
They wrapped themselves, as comrades do,
In warmth of joy, and fabric's hue.

Ties That Lead

In wacky ties, they walked the way,
Bright stripes and polka dots at play,
Each knot a wink, a cheerful tease,
As mockingbirds sang 'Take it, please!'

Through paths of quirks and jolly blues,
Their fashion sense brought forth the news,
That style can spark a silly dance,
While fate ties funny happenstance.

At every turn, they shed their fears,
With sock puppets and joyful cheers,
Each sparkle stitched in friendship's lore,
Made every day an open door.

And as the sun began to fade,
The ties still showed the fun they'd made,
A journey bright through laughter's thread,
With ties that lead where joy is spread.

Hidden Patterns

In a corner, a plaid did hide,
Unraveled from one too many slides.
Its colors clash, a bold affair,
Yet somehow, folks stop and stare.

A twisted knot, a careless fling,
Who knew that fashion could be so bling?
With stripes and dots, a sight quite rare,
It shimmies, it shakes, without a care.

Oh the tales these fabrics hold,
From awkward hugs to warmth from cold.
Each fold a story, each thread a jest,
Wrapped in laughter, life's funny quest.

So when you wrap, don't be precise,
Mix and match – your own advice!
For in the chaos, treasures lie,
A patchwork world where giggles fly.

A Tapestry of Wonders

Threads of dreams and laughable blunders,
Each stitch a tale that softly thunders.
Bizarre patterns, dizzying swirls,
To wear them proudly is for brave girls.

Knots so tight they barely breathe,
Yet everyone has their own sheathe.
Wrap them around like quirky jokes,
Each fold a laugh, each twirl invokes.

A dapper dash in a polka dot,
Who'd have thought they'd hit the spot?
With colors bright and mismatched flair,
Every twist invites a snare!

So wear your whimsy, don't be shy,
In fabric freedom, let laughter fly.
With a wink and a giggle, embrace the tease,
For every trail's just a funky breeze.

The Silk Road of Life

On this winding path, oh what a sight,
A fabric frenzy, colors bright.
Strange designs that hop and prance,
Each one whispers, 'Come take a chance!'

Silk from the east, cotton from the west,
Twisted fibers feel quite blessed.
Over yonder a taffeta tale,
With each step forward, the fun prevails.

What if I tie this bow 'round my head?
Or drape this orange where courage led?
With every knot, a dance unwinds,
Life's a runway made of funny finds.

So twirl with glee as laughter leads,
In this mishmash where joy proceeds.
For every twist, a giggle blooms,
In this wild ride of fabric fumes!

Weaving Moments

In this strange loom, moments reside,
Crafted with love, they blend and slide.
A mix of bright with shades of grey,
Curious stitches dancing away.

Each loop and whorl spins a dream,
A quilt of humor, so it seems.
With funky threads, we'd rather hug,
Than take them off, just a silly tug!

We wear our tales, a patchwork show,
Of laughter woven, row by row.
The more bizarre, the better we feel,
In this tapestry, we reveal.

So grab a thread, join the fun,
Life's a riot when we come undone.
In every weave, a chuckle waits,
Embrace the quirky, don't hesitate!

The Fabric of Fortuity

In a town where socks went roam,
A scarf took flight, far from home.
With quirky stripes and dots so bright,
It tangled dreams on a starry night.

It snatched a cat with dazzling flair,
Who twirled and danced without a care.
The neighbors laughed at the silly sight,
A fabric flurry, a pure delight.

A pigeon perched, with style so grand,
Wrapped in threads, he took a stand.
He cooed a tune, oh what a thrill,
As laughter echoed down the hill.

So if you see a scarf take flight,
Just wave hello, it's quite a sight.
For chance can weave a tale so sweet,
Where threads collide and laughter greets.

Stitched Encounters

A wandering scarf with tales to share,
Met a hat with a flair so rare.
Together they danced on the city street,
Creating a ruckus, their moves upbeat.

A dog scooped by in a furry chase,
Tangled the duo with silly grace.
They laughed and twirled, a mismatched crew,
Stitched by fate, they painted the view.

A ladybug joined with a bouncy hop,
"O, what fun! Let's never stop!"
In this mad swirl of colors and laughs,
They stitched together their charming paths.

As night descended with stars aglow,
They shared stories in a gentle flow.
So if you find a cap or a thread,
Know in each encounter, joy is spread.

Tangles of Fate

Two socks in a drawer could not agree,
One was polka-dotted, bold, and free.
The other was striped, quite shy, you see,
Together they laughed, both wild and free.

A rogue little thread took them for a ride,
Twisting and turning, oh, what a slide!
They bumped into gloves, all squished in a heap,
With giggles and snorts, they lost track of sleep.

A squirrel zoomed by, with a hat on his head,
"Join us, dear friends! Let's hop out of bed!"
And thus they all danced, a delightful brigade,
In a tangled soiree, memories were made.

As morning approached with a wink and a grin,
They vowed to revisit this chaos within.
For in life's funny twists, they found delight,
In the tangles of fate, every moment was bright.

Chance's Embrace

In the corner shop where oddities dwell,
A vibrant scarf rang a joyful bell.
It whispered secrets to shoes and hats,
As laughter erupted, like chittering chats.

A bee in a bowtie buzzed with glee,
"I'll join the parade, come dance with me!"
They skipped through the aisles, zigzagging away,
Mixing and mingling in a vibrant display.

An umbrella joined, quite out of place,
With sprinkles of joy on its colorful lace.
They twirled 'neath the lights and made quite a scene,
In a whimsical world where chaos is keen.

So when you encounter a misfit or two,
Remember the joy that's waiting for you.
In chance's embrace, let your spirit soar,
For laughter and friendship can always restore.

Auroras of Opportunity

In a closet of colors, bright and bizarre,
Hides the warmth of a life, never too far.
Each twist and turn, a mishap in time,
Worn with laughter, idiotic yet sublime.

I wrapped it around, hoping for flair,
Got tangled instead, what a sight, I swear!
The neighbors all chuckle, pointing and grinning,
Yet somehow I feel like I'm always winning.

When droplets of rain start to fall all around,
I wear it like armor, I'm not feeling down.
A rogue gust of wind pulls me this way and that,
A dance of calamity, I tip, then I flap.

Yet through all the zany, a lesson unfurls,
In the threads of the funny, life gives us pearls.
So here's to the goof-ups, the mishaps, the glee,
Where every wild turn leads to joy, don't you see?

Patterns Beneath the Surface

The fabric's a tangle, a riot of hues,
With polka dots, stripes, and some quirky old blues.
Each loop has a story, each weave is a joke,
As I trip on my shoelace, my hopes start to choke.

Choosing the wildest, ignoring the sense,
I stroll with the flair of a circus immense.
Seagulls are laughing, they're pecking at me,
But I tie it all snazzy, just wait and see.

In a world of the silly, I waddle and spin,
My fashion is chaos, where awkwardness wins.
"I own this," I say, as I trip on a sock,
The crowd goes wild—oh, the joy of the mock.

Patterns get messier, but I'm learning to thrive,
In the giggles and blunders, I'm truly alive.
So let's twist and shout in this huddle of fun,
With every misstep, it's a win that's just begun.

Cords of Complexity

Knots and loops, what a tangled affair,
I wear it like a champ with a flip of my hair.
A drone buzzing by, I think it's my friend,
But I run into walls, and the mishaps won't end.

With each little twist, I might lose my way,
But hey, isn't laughter the light of the day?
As I trip on the hem, and laugh till I cry,
The universe chuckles, and so do I.

Stitching confusion in threads of delight,
I hop like a rabbit, my pants are too tight.
Yet flailing like this, I discover the sport,
In chaos and giggles, I find my consort.

Oh, cords of complexity, what a sly gift,
A tangle of happenings, a whimsical lift.
Embrace every snap, every dash, every reel,
In the craft of the whirl, find the joy that you feel.

Spun from the Ordinary

Daily routine, oh, how mundane it seems,
But watch as I turn it, igniting those dreams.
With curls of a wisp and a wink of the eye,
I twirl up the street, letting giggles fly high.

Coffee shop chatter, the laughter is loud,
Where clumsy encounters attract a small crowd.
I trip on a chair, a stumble, a smile,
The world is a stage—let's dance for a while.

Cinnamon bun, oh, look what I've done!
A twist of the pastry becomes quite the fun.
Every bite's an adventure, each crumb a delight,
As I parade through the chaos, I feel so light.

From the routine to the wacky, I take it all in,
These threads of the ordinary invite mischief and sin.
So here's to the moments of laughter and glee,
For the quirky and odd are the best parts of me.

The Whispering Web

In a closet, colors clash,
Where mismatched patterns love to splash,
A scarf unfolds, with a sassy twist,
And ties itself into a sticky fist.

The cat jumps high, swipes with glee,
As I trip over yarn, oh dear me!
Each loop a giggle, a tangle of fun,
Who knew wardrobe chaos could be so pun?

A vibrant swirl, a sneeze of fate,
Knotting together like a dinner plate,
Friends come by and chuckle loud,
At this wild art I wear so proud!

So here's to fashion, unplanned and free,
Where every twist tells a tale of spree,
With laughter sewn in each colorful thread,
My closet's a circus, I'm the clown instead!

Luscious Twists

In a world of colors bold and bright,
My adventure starts with fabric's flight,
A noodle of silk, a ribbon of cheer,
Woven together, oh what a weird sphere!

The mirror giggles, showing my flair,
With a loop on my head, I'm a modern heir!
A dip and a twirl, I try to pose,
But end up wrapped like a garden hose.

My neighbors peek out, with raised brows,
'What's that fashion? Where's the wow?'
I give them a wink, a grandiose spin,
"Just fluffing my style, let the fun begin!"

So here I prance, in joyful distress,
A swirl of designs, embracing the mess,
With every tangle, I dance with delight,
In a luscious twist, I own the night!

An Unexpected Tangle

Strolling through life, with flair and zest,
I spy a fabric, bold and blessed,
A playful knot, a whirl of cheer,
But who's laughing now? Oh dear, oh dear!

Threads intertwine, a dance of fate,
Like spaghetti dreams on a dinner plate,
I skip and I slide, but it's not a game,
Now I'm captured in a textural frame!

My friend's on the floor, rolling with glee,
As I wrestle this ribbon that won't set free,
"Fashion's a struggle!" I declare with bite,
"An artful entanglement, oh so bright!"

With every fuss, more laughter, more fun,
Creating a spectacle, I'm the only one,
So bring on the flares, the wild and the wack,
In this quirky tussle, there's no holding back!

Accidental Artistry

A splash of color blends with a shout,
A clutch of fabric that's twisted about,
I trip and I spin, a delightful spree,
The chaos of clothing? It's fine by me!

Balloons in the sky, what a sight to behold,
Each scarf is a story waiting to unfold,
My friends lend a hand, amidst laughter and cheer,
Creating a masterpiece, scattered here!

With every bend, I'm a fashion faux pas,
Inspired by whimsy, a traitorous star,
Stripes and polka dots, oh what a thrill,
In this accidental art, I find my will!

So here's to the mess, the funny and free,
A gallery of giggles, just look and see,
In life's tangled weave, we find our part,
Each twist and turn, a craft of the heart!

Harmonics of Happenstance

In a twist of fate, I dropped my toast,
Landed butter-side up, I cheered the most.
A cat on the fence gave me a wink,
Reminded me life's less serious than you think.

A shoe flew by, just missed my head,
Did it come from Mars or our neighbor, Fred?
With giggles in the air and music in the breeze,
I danced with the poodle; we did it with ease.

A squirrel took a leap, then fell with grace,
Claimed it was part of the acorn chase.
Life's quirks remain, and we laugh along,
In this unexpected world, we all belong.

So here's to the funny, the odd, and absurd,
To mishaps and luck, in every word.
A symphony of blunders, oh what a tune,
With laughter and joy, we'll dance till noon.

Embracing the Unexpected

Left my shoes at the door, oh what a fright,
Wore bright pink socks; they felt just right.
A dog took my sandwich, then ran down the street,
While I stood there laughing, it just couldn't be beat.

Met a penguin in town, claimed he could dance,
With a jig and a shake, he asked for a chance.
We swirled on the pavement, quite the funny sight,
Life's wild and wacky, it feels just right.

Stumbled on a turtle, named him Fast Fred,
Promised him a race, but he just shook his head.
So I ran in circles, laughed 'til I cried,
With a slow little friend, right by my side.

Every turn a twist, oh what a delight,
The unexpected moments make the heart bright.
In this circus we live, we juggle and play,
With giggles and glee, we brighten the day.

Patterns of the Serendipitous

A banana peel slipped, sent me soaring,
Landed on a trampoline, oh how I was exploring!
Bouncing with glee in a rubbery dance,
Made friends with a goldfish; we shared a glance.

A pizza slice flew; it missed my face,
But hit the town crier, oh what a disgrace!
He laughed it off, threw confetti in the air,
Suddenly the streets became a fair!

Met a man who claimed to paint with his toes,
His canvas was vibrant; it really glows.
With a splash and a dash, he covered my hat,
Now it's a masterpiece; imagine that!

With every loop and flip, life keeps us amazed,
Wander through whimsies, we stay unfazed.
In this playful realm, we twirl and we spin,
As patterns of jest make us laugh from within.

The Loom of Life

Threaded with laughter, each day we weave,
A tapestry bright, filled with tricks up our sleeve.
Colors of chaos dance all around,
In this funny old patchwork, joy is found.

I met a wise chicken, told me a joke,
Said, 'Don't count your eggs, just take a poke!'
With feathers so bright and a wink in her eye,
She spread cheer and giggles, oh my, oh my!

A sock puppet brigade was marching in line,
Declaring a festival, purely divine.
They juggled spaghetti and did a soft shoe,
In this world of whimsy, odd friendships ensue.

In the loom of our days, what a weave we create,
With amusing encounters, oh how they relate!
So let's spin our tales, with laughter bestowed,
In this funny old journey, we share the road.

Fabricated Fortunes

In a shop where fortunes weave,
Lies a fabric that makes one believe.
Striped with laughter, polka-dots bright,
It dazzles and twirls, oh what a sight!

A thread of luck or a stitch of fate,
Every turn brings reason to celebrate.
I wore it once; tripped on my shoe,
Now I'm the clown in this colorful zoo!

The weaver grins, what a clever chap,
Sewed mischief and magic into each flap.
With every twist, there's chaos and cheer,
Fate's funny fabric, let's all grab a beer!

So, if it unravels, don't be dismayed,
Wrap it around and let laughs cascade.
For in this tangle, joy tightly nestles,
Life's wild designs keep us on our vessels!

A Serendipitous Wrap

Once wrapped in a bundle of bright hues,
I found myself locked in mismatched shoes.
The universe giggled, ripped at the seams,
As I pranced around fulfilling my dreams.

A twist of the fabric led me astray,
Found a lost sock on my leg, oh hooray!
Whirling in circles, I danced with delight,
Every slip was a giggle, brought pure fright!

Matching my outfit with chaotic flair,
The mirror just chuckled; who really would care?
What's fashion but laughter, a whimsical game,
With this trusty wrap, I feel no shame.

So dance through the fabric, bounce back to fate,
Where every mishap becomes something great.
In this joyful embrace, life's quirks we adopt,
With every misstep, let's laugh till we're dropped!

Fragments of Fateful Threads

A spool of confusion sat on the shelf,
It whispered to me, 'Come play with yourself!'
With threads that giggle at every wrong knot,
I tightened my grip; oh, what a hot spot!

I stitched together a whimsical fate,
But my blouse seemed to flinch; oh, it wasn't too late.
The pattern was off, yet the colors were bold,
Sometimes the fabric's the story retold!

Rags that were tattered, once dull and gray,
Now flurry with laughter and funky display.
In a patchwork of nonsense, I jumped and I spun,
Who knew that a mishap could be so much fun?

If fate gives you fabrics that twist and entwine,
Wrap 'em around till you're feeling divine.
Don a coat of jest, let your worries drift,
In this giggly mess, find your playful gift!

The Cloak of Curiosity

A cloak of wonder, stitches askew,
What's that hiding, peeking at you?
With pockets of secrets, a giggle or two,
Each fold hides laughter, cozy and new.

I wandered the market, pulled the strings tight,
Lost in the fray, what a funny sight!
Every turn led to a curious tale,
Where socks become hats and muffins set sail!

Embracing the chaos, oh what a thrill,
The fabric it whispers, 'Adventure is real.'
So wrap yourself warmly in mischief and cheer,
In this cloak of oddities, there's nothing to fear!

From snags to surprises, let curiosities play,
In this patchwork of life, we laugh all the way.
For every odd twist is a party on the street,
With the cloak of delight, how could we ever retreat?

Serendipitous Weavings

Threaded paths that twist and turn,
Lost in laughter, we discern.
A sock began to lose its mate,
Yet in the drawer, we find a great.

Fortunes worn upon our backs,
Bumpy rides and missing snacks.
A tangle here, a fumble there,
Who knew joy was hiding, rare?

Patterns formed from happy chance,
Each mishap starts a merry dance.
From chaos springs a lively thread,
With every loop, new tales are fed.

So come and join this quirky spree,
In every knot, a mystery.
We weave together joy and glee,
In every stitch, our lives agree.

The Shawl of Surprise

A shawl drapes over clumsy shoulders,
Hiding secrets and forgotten boulders.
It flutters wildly, a playful tease,
Wrapped in whimsy, enough to please.

Each fold holds tales of unexpected gains,
Like finding lost keys on the window panes.
It slips and slides, like life's own game,
In tangled messes, we find our fame.

Laughter erupts at the silliest sights,
As grandma's shawl takes mysterious flights.
Whirling like a dervish, it leads the way,
Embracing chaos in a jolly ballet.

With every sweep, hearts grow bold,
In this fabric are stories untold.
Wear it proudly, let laughter ring,
For joy's a tune, and this shawl can sing!

Hues of Happenstance

Colorful threads in a jumbled row,
The mix match wonders put on a show.
A pop of red where blue once laid,
In this fabric, no plans were made.

Surprises bloom like clowns at a fair,
Each glance a chuckle, we've got flair.
With stripes and dots, a palette absurd,
From mayhem's art, we find the word.

A playful swirl of joy's own brush,
On the canvas of life, we blend and rush.
With every hue, a quirky smile,
Fate intervenes, and we go wild.

In vibrant chaos, moments ignite,
Painting laughter in colors bright.
So throw on mischief, let spirits fly,
In this happy tapestry, oh my!

A Tapestry of Moments

Woven stories, a curious blend,
With each twist, a new friend.
A mishap turns to a brilliant turn,
In this fabric, we laugh and learn.

Each patch recalls a moment cheesy,
With wisecracks shared, never too easy.
A clumsy spin, a daring dash,
When serendipity sings, we clash!

The loom of life invites the odd,
With threads of joy, no need for a prod.
In mishaps, we find our tale to spin,
A tapestry of laughter, where do we begin?

So gather 'round and take a glance,
In this funny quilt, we shall dance.
Celebrate the quirks, embrace the jest,
In the tapestry of life, we're all blessed!

www.ingramcontent.com/pod-product-compliance
Lightning Source LLC
Chambersburg PA
CBHW070312120526
44590CB00017B/2639